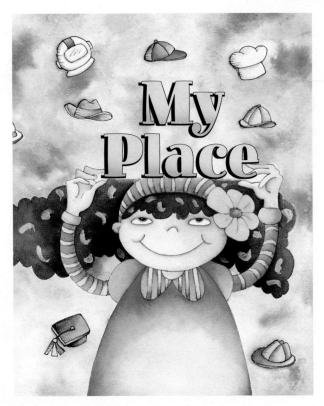

by F. Isabel Campoy
illustrated by Enrique Martinez

Orlando   Boston   Dallas   Chicago   San Diego

Visit *The Learning Site!*

www.harcourtschool.com

Everywhere I look, I find people who have special places. Each person has a special thing to do. Each person has a special place to work.

An astronaut has a special place. He or she works in a space shuttle. An astronaut may walk on the moon! What is it like to walk on the moon?

A soccer player has a special place. He or she plays on a soccer field. A soccer player runs and kicks a ball. What is it like to score a goal?

A gardener has a special place. He or she works in a garden. A gardener takes care of growing plants. What is it like to watch a flower bloom?

An actor has a special place. He or she performs in a play on a stage. An actor has to remember a lot of lines. What is it like to act on a stage?

A doctor has a special place. He
or she helps people in a hospital. A
doctor fixes broken bones and listens
to hearts. What does a heartbeat
sound like?

A gymnast has a special place. He or she does cartwheels and flips in a gym. A gymnast has to have good balance. What is it like to walk on a balance beam?

A baker has a special place. He or
she bakes bread and cakes in a bakery.
A baker knows how to make many
kinds of bread. What does fresh-baked
bread smell like?

A runner has a special place. He or she runs races on a track. A runner has to be healthy to run fast. What is it like to win a race?

A fisher has a special place. He
or she sails in a boat on the ocean.
A fisher catches lots of fresh fish.
What is it like to sail on the ocean?

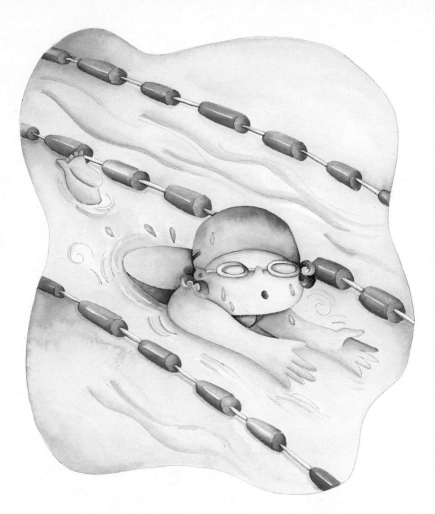

A swimmer has a special place. He or she swims in a swimming pool. A swimmer must have strong arms and legs. What is it like to glide through cool water?

A crossing guard has a special
place. He or she works at a busy
corner near a school. A crossing guard
helps children cross the street safely.
What is it like to stop all that traffic?

A teacher has a special place. He or she helps students in a classroom. A teacher answers questions all day long. What is it like to know so much information?

I have a special place, too. My
special place is my school. I can try
new things there without being afraid.
What new things will I try today?

Look around. You will find people
who have special places. You have a
special place, too!